Johann Sebastian
BACH

PASSACAGLIA
in C minor
BWV 582
Orchestrated by
Aleksandr Gedike
(*Richard W. Sargeant, Jr.*)

Study Score
Partitur

SERENISSIMA MUSIC, INC.

ORCHESTRA

Piccolo

2 Flutes

2 Oboes

English Horn

2 Clarinets (B-flat)

Bass Clarinet (B-flat)

2 Bassoons

Contrabasson

4 Horns (F)

3 Trumpets (B-flat)

3 Trombones

Tuba

Timpani

Percussion

(Bass Drum, Tam-Tam, Glockenspiel, Chimes)

Violin I

Violin II

Viola

Violoncello

Double Bass

Duration: ca. 15 minutes

Premiere: Unknown

ISMN: 979-0-58042-114-2
This score is a newly engraved edition based upon the
first edtion of the score issued in the USSR ca.1920.

Printed in the USA
First Printing: August, 2018

Passacaglia
in C minor
BWV 582

Johann Sebastian Bach
Arranged by Aleksandr Gedike
Edited by Richard W. Sargeant, Jr.

42264

14
17
Fl. 1 2
Ob. 1 2
Cl. 1 2
Bn. 1 2
Vn. 1
2
Va.
Vc.
Cb.
dim.
pp
div.
24
poco rit.
32 poco più mosso
1.
2.
mf
unis.

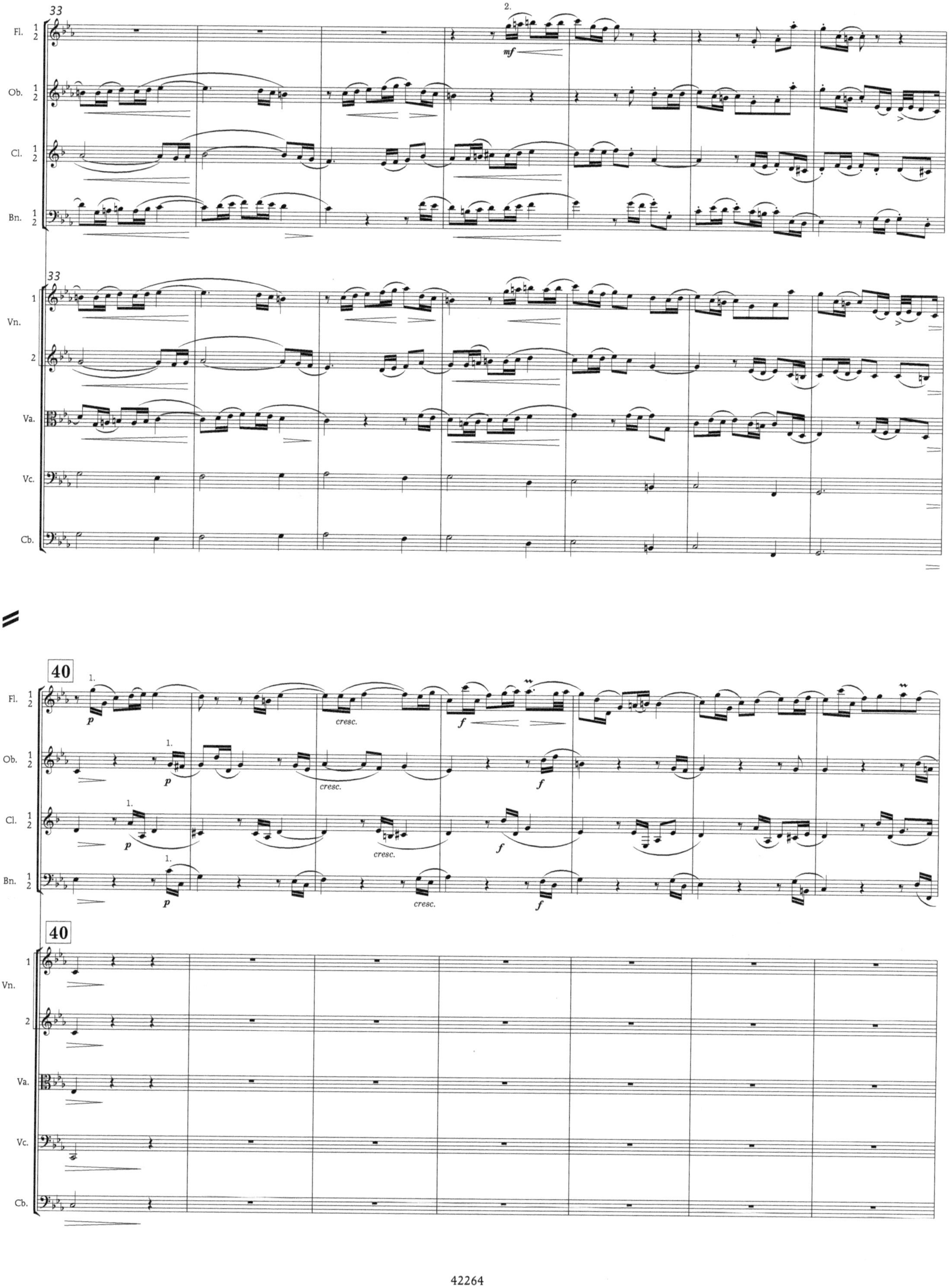
33
Fl. 1 2
Ob. 1 2
Cl. 1 2
Bn. 1 2
2.
mf
33
Vn. 1
2
Va.
Vc.
Cb.
40
1.
p
cresc.
f
40

47
48 Tempo I
Fl. 1 2
dim.
Ob. 1 2
dim.
Cl. 1 2
Bn. 1 2
p
47
48 Tempo I
solo
p
Vn. 1 2
Va.
solo
p
solo
p
Vc.
2 only
pp
Cb.
2 only
pp
53
poco rit.
56 a tempo
a2
f
a2
f
Hn. 1 2 3 4
a2
p
tutti
f
tutti
f
f
f
tutti
f

59
poco rit.
Cl. 1 2
f
Bn. 1 2
Hn. 1 2
3 4
59
poco rit.
Vn. 1
2
con sord.
Va.
con sord.
tutti
Vc.
Cb.
64
a tempo sempre sostenuto
Picc.
ppp
Fl. 1
2
Ob. 1 2
Cl. 1 2
Bn. 1 2
pp
Cbn.
Hn. 1 2
3 4
64
a tempo sempre sostenuto
con sord.
Vn. 1
2
pp
ppp
Va.
Vc.
Cb.

rall.
72 Allegro moderato ♩ = 63
69
Picc.
Fl.
Ob.
Cl.
B. Cl.
Bn.
a2
Cbn.
Hn.
Tpt.
Trb.
Tuba
f
Timp.
B. D
T.-t.
Glock.
Chim.
Vn.
Va.
Vc.
Cb.
senza sord.

74
Picc.
Fl. 1 2
Ob. 1 2
Cl. 1 2
B. Cl.
Bn. 1 2
Cbn.
Hn. 1 2 3 4
Tpt. 1 2 3
a2
Trb. 1 2 3
Tuba
Timp.
B. D
T.-t.
Glock.
Chim.
74
Vn. 1 2
Va.
Vc.
Cb.

poco rit.
80
a tempo
79
Picc.
Fl. 1 2
Ob. 1 2
Cl. 1 2
B. Cl.
Bn. 1 2
Cbn.
Hn. 1 2 3 4
Tpt. 1 2 3
Trb. 1 2 3
Tuba
Timp.
B. D
T.-t.
Glock.
Chim.
Vn. 1 2
Va.
Vc.
Cb.
ff
f
mf

84
Picc.
ff
Fl. 1 2
Ob. 1 2
1.
p espress.
Cl. 1 2
B. Cl.
Bn. 1 2
Cbn.
Hn. 1 2
3 4
Tpt. 1 2
3
Trb. 1 2
3
Tuba
Timp.
B. D
T.-t.
Glock.
Chim.
84
Vn. 1
2
Va.
Vc.
p
Cb.

89

97 a tempo (Allegro moderato e energico)

95 poco rit.

97 a tempo (Allegro moderato e energico)

95 poco rit.

100
poco rit.
Picc.
Fl. 1 2
Ob. 1 2
Cl. 1 2
Bn. 1 2
Cbn.
Hn. 1 2 3 4
p
Vn. 1 2
Va.
Vc.
Cb.
p espress.
105
1.
Ob. 1 2
Hn. 1 2 3 4
Vn. 1 2
Va.
Vc.
Cb.
p espress.

113
rall.
a tempo
111
Fl.
Ob.
Cl.
B. Cl.
Hn.
Vn.
Va.
Vc.
Cb.
pizz.
poco rit.
120
a tempo
117
arco

123
Picc.
Fl. 1 2
Ob. 1 2
Cl. 1 2
B. Cl.
Bn. 1 2
Cbn.
Hn. 1 2
3 4
Tpt. 1 2
3
Trb. 1 2
3
Tuba
Timp.
B. D
T.-t.
Glock.
Chim.
123
Vn. 1
2
Va.
arco
pizz.
Vc.
Cb.

129
rit.
a tempo, maestoso
128
Picc.
Fl.
Ob.
Cl.
B. Cl.
Bn.
Cbn.
Hn.
Tpt.
Trb.
Tuba
Timp.
B. D
T.-t.
Glock.
Chim.
a2
ff
f
mf
Vn.
Va.
Vc.
Cb.
arco

133
Picc.
ff
Fl. 1 2
Ob. 1 2
Cl. 1 2
B. Cl.
Bn. 1 2
Cbn.
Hn. 1 2 3 4
a2
mf
Tpt. 1 2 3
Trb. 1 2 3
Tuba
Timp.
B. D
T.-t.
Glock.
Chim.
133
Vn. 1 2
Va.
Vc.
Cb.
f

137
Picc.
a2
Fl. 1 2
Ob. 1 2
Cl. 1 2
B. Cl.
Bn. 1 2
Cbn.
Hn. 1 2 3 4
Tpt. 1 2 3
Trb. 1 2 3
Tuba
Timp.
B. D
T.-t.
Glock.
Chim.
137
Vn. 1 2
Va.
Vc.
Cb.
f

140
Picc.
Fl. 1 2
Ob. 1 2
Cl. 1 2
B. Cl.
Bn. 1 2
Cbn.
Hn. 1 2 3 4
Tpt. 1 2 3
Trb. 1 2 3
Tuba
Timp.
B. D
T.-t.
Glock.
Chim.
140
Vn. 1 2
Va.
Vc.
Cb.

144
145
Picc.
Fl. 1 2
Ob. 1 2
Cl. 1 2
B. Cl.
Bn. 1 2
Cbn.
Hn. 1 2
3 4
Tpt. 1 2
3
Trb. 1 2
3 Tuba
Timp.
B. D T.-t.
Glock.
Chim.
Vn. 1
2
Va.
Vc.
Cb.
ff
f

151
153
Picc.
Fl. 1 2
Ob. 1 2
a2
ff
p subito
cresc. poco a poco
Cl. 1 2
B. Cl.
Bn. 1 2
Cbn.
Hn. 1 2
Hn. 3 4
Tpt. 1 2
Tpt. 3
Trb. 1 2
Trb. 3 Tuba
Tuba
Timp.
B. D T.-t.
Glock.
Chim.
Vn. 1
Vn. 2
Va.
Vc.
Cb.

161 Sostenuto

158

Picc.

Fl. 1 2

Ob. 1 2

Cl. 1 2

B. Cl.

Bn. 1 2

Cbn.

Hn. 1 2

3 4

Tpt. 1 2

3

Trb. 1 2

3
Tuba

Timp.

B. D
T.-t.

Glock.

Chim.

161 Sostenuto

158

Vn. 1

2

Va.

Vc.

Cb.

molto rall.

* after the cutoff for the fermata in the orchestral tutti, the 1st bassoon continues holding into the start of the following fugato.

169 Thema fugatum ♩ = 63
Fl. 1 2
Ob. 1 2
Cl. 1 2
Bn. 1 2
1.
p
169 Thema fugatum ♩ = 63
Vn. 1 2
Va.
Vc.
Cb.
unis.
pp
176
179

182
Picc.
Fl. 1 2
Ob. 1 2
Cl. 1 2
1.
p cresc.
B. Cl.
Bn. 1 2
Cbn.
Hn. 1 2
3 4
Tpt. 1 2
3
Trb. 1 2
a2
pp cresc.
mp
3 Tuba
3.
pp cresc.
mp
Timp.
B. D T.-t.
Glock.
Chim.
182
Vn. 1
2
cresc.
mf
Va.
p cresc.
mf
Vc.
cresc.
mf
Cb.
cresc.
mf

191
188
Picc.
Fl.
Ob.
Cl.
B. Cl.
Bn.
Cbn.
Hn.
Tpt.
Trb.
Tuba
Timp.
B. D
T.-t.
Glock.
Chim.
Vn.
Va.
Vc.
Cb.
1.
a2
mf
f
p

194
197
Fl. 1 2
Ob. 1 2
Cl. 1 2
B. Cl.
Bn. 1 2
Hn. 1 2 3 4
Vn. 1 2
Va.
Vc.
Cb.
a2
f
p
1.
pp
dim.
200

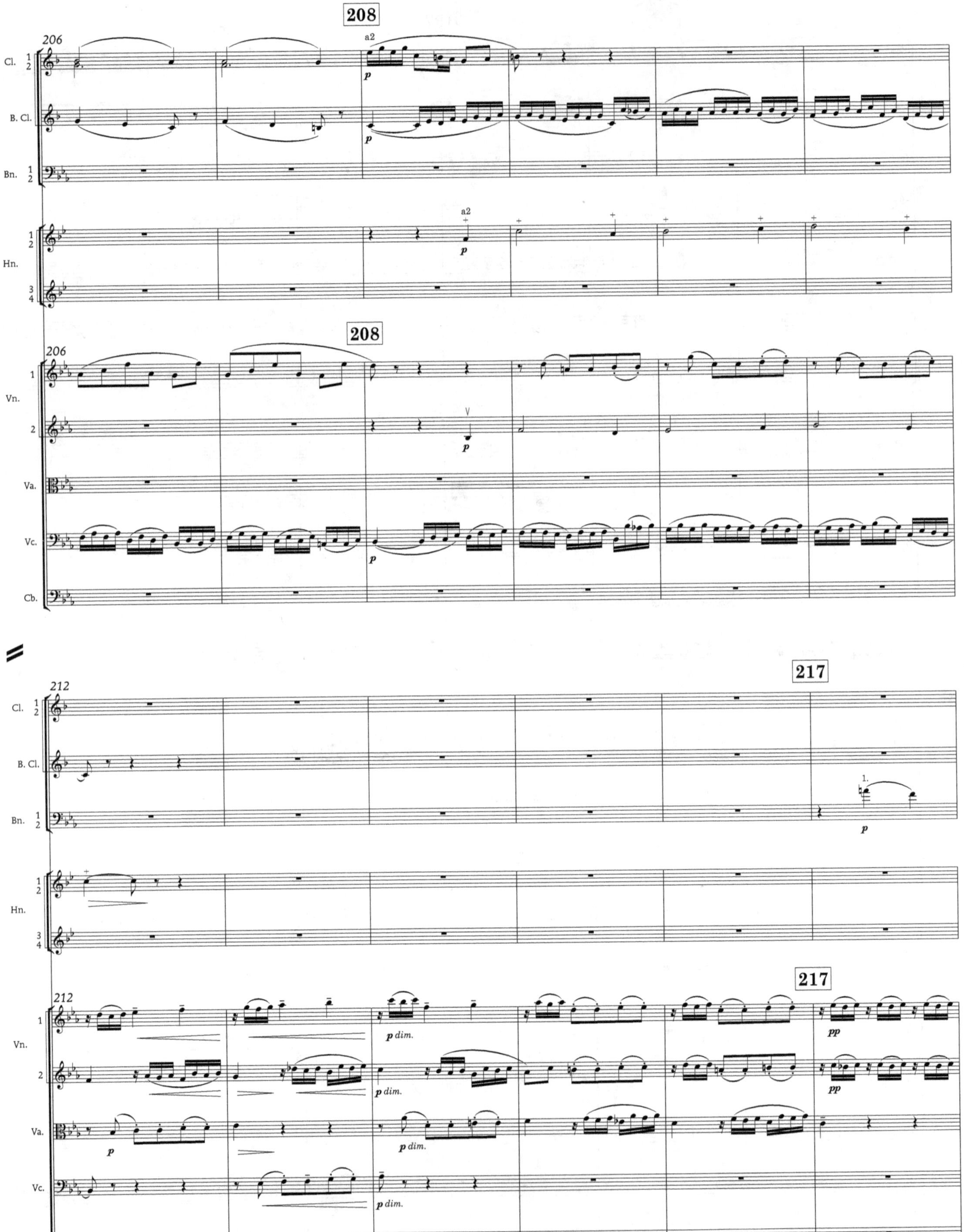
208
206
Cl. 1 2
B. Cl.
Bn. 1 2
Hn. 1 2
3 4
a2
p
Vn. 1
2
Va.
Vc.
Cb.
212
217
1.
p dim.
pp

218
Picc.
Fl. 1 2
1.
p
cresc.
Ob. 1 2
Cl. 1 2
1.
p
cresc.
B. Cl.
p
cresc.
Bn. 1 2
a2
p
cresc.
Cbn.
Hn. 1 2
3 4
Tpt. 1 2
3
Trb. 1 2
3 Tuba
Timp.
B. D T.-t.
Glock.
Chim.
218
Vn. 1
p
cresc.
2
p
Va.
p
cresc.
Vc.
1 desk
p
cresc.
tutti
p
cresc.
Cb.
p
cresc.

224
225
Picc.
Fl. 1 2
Ob. 1 2
Cl. 1 2
a2
mf
B. Cl.
Bn. 1 2
mf
Cbn.
Hn. 1 2
3 4
Tpt. 1 2
3
Trb. 1 2
3 Tuba
Timp.
B. D T.-t.
Glock.
Chim.
224
225
Vn. 1
2
mf
Va.
mf
Vc.
mf
mf
Cb.
mf

230
232
Picc.
Fl. 1 2
1.
mf cresc.
Ob. 1 2
Cl. 1 2
1.
mf cresc.
B. Cl.
Bn. 1 2
Cbn.
Hn. 1 2
3 4
Tpt. 1 2
3
Trb. 1 2
a2
p
cresc.
3 Tuba
Timp.
B. D
T.-t.
Glock.
Chim.
230
232
Vn. 1
2
mf
mf
Va.
mf
Vc.
mf
mf
Cb.
mf

239
236
Picc.
Fl.
Ob.
mf cresc.
f cresc.
Cl.
B. Cl.
f
Bn.
Cbn.
a2
Hn.
Tpt.
Trb.
Tuba
Timp.
B. D
T.-t.
Glock.
Chim.
239
236
Vn.
Va.
unis.
Vc.
Cb.
f cresc.

242
Picc.
Fl. 1 2
Ob. 1 2
Cl. 1 2
B. Cl.
Bn. 1 2
Cbn.
Hn. 1 2
3 4
Tpt. 1 2
3
Trb. 1 2
3 Tuba
Timp.
B. D T.-t.
Glock.
Chim.
242
Vn. 1
2
Va.
Vc.
Cb.
a2
ff

247
Picc.
Fl. 1 2
Ob. 1 2
Cl. 1 2
B. Cl.
Bn. 1 2
Cbn.
a2
Hn. 1 2 3 4
ff
Tpt. 1 2 3
Trb. 1 2
3 Tuba
Timp.
B. D
T.-t.
Glock.
Chim.
247
Vn. 1 2
Va.
Vc.
Cb.

252
Picc.
Fl. 1 2
Ob. 1 2
Cl. 1 2
B. Cl.
Bn. 1 2
a2
Cbn.
Hn. 1 2 3 4
Tpt. 1 2 3
f
Trb. 1 2
a2
mf
3 Tuba
Timp.
B. D T.-t.
Glock.
Chim.
252
Vn. 1 2
Va.
Vc.
ff
Cb.

258
257
Picc.
Fl. 1 2
Ob. 1 2
Cl. 1 2
B. Cl.
Bn. 1 2
Cbn.
Hn. 1 2
3 4
1.
mf
Tpt. 1 2
3
Trb. 1 2
3 Tuba
Timp.
B. D T.-t.
Glock.
Chim.
258
257
Vn. 1
2
Va.
Vc.
Cb.

262
Picc.
Fl. 1 2
Ob. 1 2
Cl. 1 2
B. Cl.
Bn. 1 2
Cbn.
Hn. 1 2 3 4
Tpt. 1 2 3
Trb. 1 2 3
Tuba
Timp.
B. D
T.-t.
Glock.
Chim.
Vn. 1 2
Va.
Vc.
Cb.
1.
3.
mf
f

268
269
Picc.
Fl. 1 2
Ob. 1 2
Cl. 1 2
B. Cl.
Bn. 1 2
Cbn.
Hn. 1 2
Hn. 3 4
Tpt. 1 2
Tpt. 3
Trb. 1 2
Trb. 3 Tuba
Timp.
B. D T.-t.
Glock.
Chim.
Vn. 1
Vn. 2
Va.
Vc.
Cb.
a2
ff
mf
f

273
Picc.
Fl. 1 2
Ob. 1 2
Cl. 1 2
B. Cl.
Bn. 1 2
Cbn.
Hn. 1 2 3 4
Tpt. 1 2 3
Trb. 1 2 3
Tuba
Timp.
B. D
T.-t.
Glock.
Chim.
273
Vn. 1 2
Va.
div.
Vc.
Cb.
f
p

281 allargando
278
Picc.
Fl. 1 2
Ob. 1 2
a2
Cl. 1 2
B. Cl.
Bn. 1 2
Cbn.
Hn. 1 2
3 4
Tpt. 1 2
3
Trb. 1 2
3 Tuba
Timp.
B. D T.-t.
Glock.
Chim.
Vn. 1
2
Va.
Vc.
Cb.
cresc.
f cresc.
ff

283
ritenuto
288
a tempo sostenuto
Picc.
Fl. 1 2
Ob. 1 2
Cl. 1 2
B. Cl.
Bn. 1 2
Cbn.
Hn. 1 2
3 4
Tpt. 1 2
3
Trb. 1 2
3 Tuba
Timp.
B. D T.-t.
Glock.
Chim.
fff
ff sempre
a2
ff
f
p
Vn. 1
2
Va.
Vc.
div.
Cb.

rit poco a poco
Adagio
289
Picc.
Fl. 1 2
Ob. 1 2
Cl. 1 2
B. Cl.
Bn. 1 2
a2
Cbn.
Hn. 1 2
3 4
Tpt. 1 2
3
Trb. 1 2
3 Tuba
Timp.
ff
B. D T.-t.
f
Glock.
Chim.
rit poco a poco
Adagio
289
div.
div.
Vn. 1
2
Va.
Vc.
Cb.